Success With

Math Tests

Editor: Ourania Papacharalambous
Educational consultant: Michael Priestley
Cover design by Tannaz Fassihi; cover illustration by Kevin Zimmer
Interior design by Michelle H. Kim
Interior illustrations by Kate Flanagan; Doug Jones (3, 23)
All other images © Shutterstock.com.

ISBN 978-1-338-79844-9
Scholastic Inc., 557 Broadway, New York, NY 10012
Copyright © 2022 Scholastic Inc.
All rights reserved. Printed in the U.S.A.
First printing, January 2022
1 2 3 4 5 6 7 8 9 10   40   29 28 27 26 25 24 23 22

TABLE OF CONTENTS

INTRODUCTION

In this book, you will find eight Practice Tests designed to help students prepare to take standardized tests. Each test has multiple-choice items that closely resemble the kinds of questions students will have to answer on "real" tests. Each test will take 30–40 minutes for students to complete.

The math skills measured in these tests and the types of questions are based on detailed analyses and correlations of widely used standardized tests and the curriculum standards measured by many statewide tests.

How to Use the Tests

Tell students how much time they will have to complete the test. Encourage them to work quickly and carefully and to keep track of the remaining time—just as they would in a real testing session. You may have students mark their answers directly on the test pages, or you may have them use a copy of the **Answer Sheet**. An answer sheet appears at the end of each test. The answer sheet will help students become accustomed to filling in bubbles on a real test. It may also make the tests easier for you to score.

We do not recommend the use of calculators. For Practice Tests 2 and 6, students will need an inch ruler and a centimeter ruler to answer some of the questions.

At the back of this book, you will find **Tested Skills** charts and **Answer Keys** for the eight Practice Tests. The Tested Skills charts list the skills measured in each test and the test questions that measure each skill. These charts may be helpful to you in determining what kinds of questions students answered incorrectly, what skills they may be having trouble with, and who may need further instruction in particular skills. To score a Practice Test, refer to the Answer Key for that test. The Answer Key lists the correct response to each question.

To score a Practice Test, go through the test and mark each question answered correctly. Add the total number of questions answered correctly to find the student's test score. To find a percentage score, divide the number answered correctly by the total number of questions. For example, the percentage score for a student who answers 20 out of 25 questions correctly is 20 ÷ 25 = 0.80, or 80%. You might want to have students correct their own tests. This will give them a chance to see where they made mistakes and what they need to do to improve their scores on the next test.

On the next page of this book, you will find **Test-Taking Tips**. You may want to share these tips and strategies with students before they begin working on the Practice Tests.

TEST-TAKING TIPS: MATHEMATICS

1 For each test, read the directions carefully so you know what to do. Then, read the directions again—just to make sure.

2 Look for key words and phrases to help you decide what each question is asking and what kind of computation you need to do. Examples of key words: *less than, greatest, least, farther, longest, divided equally.*

3 To help solve a problem, write a number sentence or equation.

4 Use scrap paper (or extra space on the test page) to write down the numbers and information you need to solve a problem.

5 If a question has a picture or diagram, study it carefully. Draw your own picture or diagram if it will help you solve a problem.

6 Try to solve each problem before you look at the answer choices. (In some tests, the correct answer may not be given, so you will want to be sure of your answer. In these tests, questions use "NG" for "Not Given.")

7 Check your work carefully before you finish. (For many questions, you can check your answer by working backwards to see if the numbers work out correctly.)

8 If you are not sure which answer is correct, cross out every answer that you know is wrong. Then make your best guess.

9 To complete a number sentence or equation, try all the answer choices until you find the one that works.

10 When working with fractions, always reduce (or rename) the fractions to their lowest parts. When working with decimals, keep the decimal points lined up correctly.

Name _____   Date _____

Practice Test 1: Numeration and Number Concepts

Directions. Choose the best answer to each question. Mark your answer.

1 Becky was counting the children in a line.

> 2, 4, 6, 8, ___

Which number should come next?

Ⓐ 9
Ⓑ 10
Ⓒ 11
Ⓓ 12

2 There are **10** pencils in each bundle.

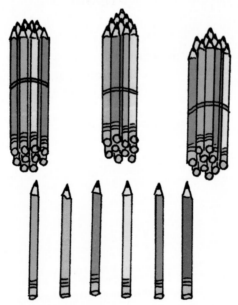

How many pencils are there in all?

Ⓐ 9
Ⓑ 30
Ⓒ 35
Ⓓ 36

3 The Nile River is four thousand one hundred sixty miles long. Which number means four thousand one hundred sixty?

Ⓐ 40,160
Ⓑ 4106
Ⓒ 4016
Ⓓ 4160

4 Great Bear Lake is **1463** feet deep. What is that number in words?

Ⓐ one hundred four sixty-three
Ⓑ one thousand forty-six three
Ⓒ one thousand four hundred sixty-three
Ⓓ ten thousand four hundred sixty-three

5 Which teacher has an odd number of students in his or her class?

Ⓐ Mrs. Bennet   27
Ⓑ Ms. Bradford   22
Ⓒ Mrs. Alexander 30
Ⓓ Mr. Collins   28

GO ON

Practice Test 1 *(continued)*

6 The chart shows the number of people who live in each town.

Town	Number of People
Ascot	804
Grant	791
Stoneham	845
Wardsboro	973

Which town has the least number of people?

Ⓐ Ascot
Ⓑ Grant
Ⓒ Stoneham
Ⓓ Wardsboro

7 Which number means

$$5000 + 60 + 8 \ ?$$

Ⓐ 568
Ⓑ 5068
Ⓒ 5608
Ⓓ 50,608

8 Mr. Evans drove **3295** miles last month. What is that number rounded to the nearest hundred?

Ⓐ 3000
Ⓑ 3200
Ⓒ 3300
Ⓓ 4000

9 Wanda is making a bead necklace with this pattern.

If this pattern continues, what will the next two beads look like?

Ⓐ
Ⓑ
Ⓒ
Ⓓ

10 Mr. Craig wrote this number pattern on the whiteboard.

3, 7, 11, 15, ___

If the same pattern continues, what should the next number be?

Ⓐ 16
Ⓑ 18
Ⓒ 19
Ⓓ 20

11 Which street has an even number?

Ⓐ 27 Street
Ⓑ 39 Street
Ⓒ 15 Street
Ⓓ 48 Street

GO ON

Practice Test 1 *(continued)*

12 On Monday, **715** people went to the mall. On Tuesday, **892** people went to the mall. <u>About</u> how many people went to the mall in those two days?

Ⓐ 1200
Ⓑ 1400
Ⓒ 1600
Ⓓ 1800

13 What number is shown on the number line?

Ⓐ 203
Ⓑ 213
Ⓒ 230
Ⓓ 240

14 Jeremy had **$104.00** in the bank. He took out **$47.00** to buy a video game. <u>About</u> how much money did he have left?

Ⓐ $25.00
Ⓑ $50.00
Ⓒ $80.00
Ⓓ $100.00

15 Which is another way to write

$$4 + 4 + 4 + 4 + 4 ?$$

Ⓐ $4 + 5$
Ⓑ $4 \times 4 \times 4 \times 4 \times 4$
Ⓒ $20 + 4$
Ⓓ 4×5

16 Willy has **8** markers of different colors.

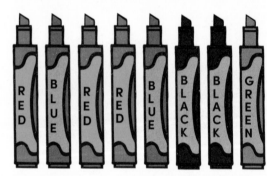

What fractional part of the markers are red?

Ⓐ $\frac{1}{4}$

Ⓑ $\frac{3}{5}$

Ⓒ $\frac{1}{2}$

Ⓓ $\frac{3}{8}$

GO ON ➡

Practice Test 1 (continued)

17 Which figure shows $\frac{2}{3}$ shaded?

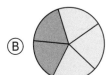 

18 Which number sentence goes with this fact?

8 + 6 = 14

Ⓐ 8 − 6 = 2
Ⓑ 14 − 6 = 8
Ⓒ 8 × 6 = 48
Ⓓ 14 + 6 = 20

19 Which box of cereal weighs most?

 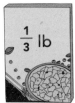 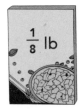

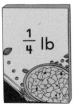 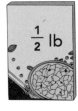

20 The chart shows how far four children hiked on a trail.

Polly	$\frac{3}{4}$ mile
Mark	$\frac{2}{5}$ mile
Stu	$\frac{1}{2}$ mile
John	$\frac{2}{3}$ mile

Which lists the four children in order from the shortest hike to the longest?

Ⓐ Polly, Mark, Stu, John
Ⓑ Mark, Stu, John, Polly
Ⓒ Stu, Mark, Polly, John
Ⓓ John, Polly, Mark, Stu

21 Which number is marked on the number line?

Ⓐ 12
Ⓑ 14
Ⓒ 15
Ⓓ 18

Answer Sheet

Student Name _____ Grade _____

Teacher Name _____ Date _____

MATHEMATICS

1 (A) (B) (C) (D) (E)   11 (A) (B) (C) (D) (E)   21 (A) (B) (C) (D) (E)
2 (A) (B) (C) (D) (E)   12 (A) (B) (C) (D) (E)   22 (A) (B) (C) (D) (E)
3 (A) (B) (C) (D) (E)   13 (A) (B) (C) (D) (E)   23 (A) (B) (C) (D) (E)
4 (A) (B) (C) (D) (E)   14 (A) (B) (C) (D) (E)   24 (A) (B) (C) (D) (E)
5 (A) (B) (C) (D) (E)   15 (A) (B) (C) (D) (E)   25 (A) (B) (C) (D) (E)
6 (A) (B) (C) (D) (E)   16 (A) (B) (C) (D) (E)   26 (A) (B) (C) (D) (E)
7 (A) (B) (C) (D) (E)   17 (A) (B) (C) (D) (E)   27 (A) (B) (C) (D) (E)
8 (A) (B) (C) (D) (E)   18 (A) (B) (C) (D) (E)   28 (A) (B) (C) (D) (E)
9 (A) (B) (C) (D) (E)   19 (A) (B) (C) (D) (E)   29 (A) (B) (C) (D) (E)
10 (A) (B) (C) (D) (E)   20 (A) (B) (C) (D) (E)   30 (A) (B) (C) (D) (E)

Practice Test 2: Geometry and Measurement

Directions. Choose the best answer to each question. Mark your answer.

1 Which unit should be used to measure how tall you are?

Ⓐ gallons

Ⓑ pounds

Ⓒ inches

Ⓓ yards

2 Marina started doing her homework at **3:15** P.M. She finished **40** minutes later. Which clock shows the time she finished?

Ⓐ    Ⓒ

Ⓑ    Ⓓ

3 Kent had these coins in his pocket. What is the total value of the coins?

Ⓐ 61¢   Ⓒ 52¢

Ⓑ 56¢   Ⓓ 51¢

This graph shows the average amount of snow that fell in four U.S. cities in the winter of **2019–2020**. Use the graph to answer questions 4 and 5.

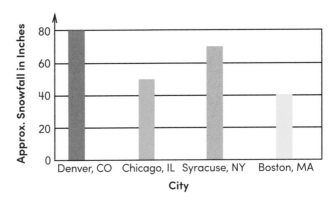

4 In which city did the greatest amount of snow fall?

Ⓐ Chicago, IL

Ⓑ Boston, MA

Ⓒ Denver, CO

Ⓓ Syracuse, NY

5 How much snow fell in Boston?

Ⓐ 40 inches

Ⓑ 50 inches

Ⓒ 70 inches

Ⓓ 80 inches

Practice Test 2 *(continued)*

6 Which part of the house has the shape of a triangle?

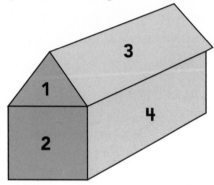

Ⓐ part 1
Ⓑ part 2
Ⓒ part 3
Ⓓ part 4

7 Each card will be folded in half on the dotted line. On which card will the two halves match exactly?

Ⓐ 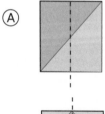   Ⓒ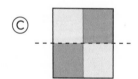

Ⓑ 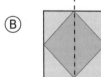   Ⓓ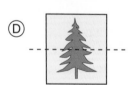

8 Which shape has 6 faces?

Ⓐ    Ⓒ

Ⓑ   Ⓓ

9 Look at Figure A.

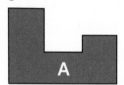

Which piece of the puzzle has the same size and shape?

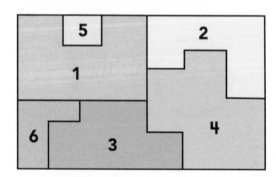

Ⓐ piece 1
Ⓑ piece 2
Ⓒ piece 3
Ⓓ piece 4

GO ON

Name _____ Date _____

Practice Test 2 *(continued)*

10 What is the area of this figure (in square units)?

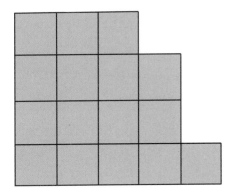

Ⓐ 16
Ⓑ 15
Ⓒ 14
Ⓓ 12

11 Where is the ★ located on the grid?

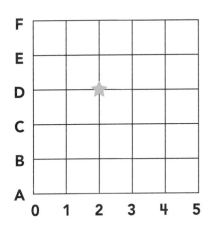

Ⓐ 2, B
Ⓑ 3, B
Ⓒ 2, D
Ⓓ 4, C

12 Matt found this money on the table.

How much money did he find?

Ⓐ $1.24
Ⓑ $1.59
Ⓒ $1.64
Ⓓ $1.80

13 What time is shown on the clock?

Ⓐ 8:15
Ⓑ 8:05
Ⓒ 1:50
Ⓓ 1:40

 GO ON

Name _____   Date _____

Practice Test 2 *(continued)*

14 If you fill a large cooking pot with water, about how much water will it hold?

Ⓐ 2 gallons
Ⓑ 20 gallons
Ⓒ 200 gallons
Ⓓ 2000 gallons

15 Which unit should be used to measure how far a school bus travels each day?

Ⓐ pounds
Ⓑ feet
Ⓒ gallons
Ⓓ miles

16 How long is the roll of mints? (Use your inch ruler.)

Ⓐ 2 inches
Ⓑ 3 inches
Ⓒ 4 inches
Ⓓ 5 inches

17 How long is the grasshopper? (Use your centimeter ruler.)

Ⓐ 4 centimeters
Ⓑ 5 centimeters
Ⓒ 6 centimeters
Ⓓ 7 centimeters

18 This box will be turned on its side in the direction of the arrow.

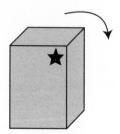

Which picture shows the box after it has been turned?

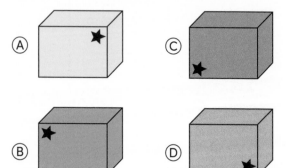

STOP

Answer Sheet

Student Name _____   Grade _____

Teacher Name _____   Date _____

MATHEMATICS

1 Ⓐ Ⓑ Ⓒ Ⓓ Ⓔ	11 Ⓐ Ⓑ Ⓒ Ⓓ Ⓔ	21 Ⓐ Ⓑ Ⓒ Ⓓ Ⓔ
2 Ⓐ Ⓑ Ⓒ Ⓓ Ⓔ	12 Ⓐ Ⓑ Ⓒ Ⓓ Ⓔ	22 Ⓐ Ⓑ Ⓒ Ⓓ Ⓔ
3 Ⓐ Ⓑ Ⓒ Ⓓ Ⓔ	13 Ⓐ Ⓑ Ⓒ Ⓓ Ⓔ	23 Ⓐ Ⓑ Ⓒ Ⓓ Ⓔ
4 Ⓐ Ⓑ Ⓒ Ⓓ Ⓔ	14 Ⓐ Ⓑ Ⓒ Ⓓ Ⓔ	24 Ⓐ Ⓑ Ⓒ Ⓓ Ⓔ
5 Ⓐ Ⓑ Ⓒ Ⓓ Ⓔ	15 Ⓐ Ⓑ Ⓒ Ⓓ Ⓔ	25 Ⓐ Ⓑ Ⓒ Ⓓ Ⓔ
6 Ⓐ Ⓑ Ⓒ Ⓓ Ⓔ	16 Ⓐ Ⓑ Ⓒ Ⓓ Ⓔ	26 Ⓐ Ⓑ Ⓒ Ⓓ Ⓔ
7 Ⓐ Ⓑ Ⓒ Ⓓ Ⓔ	17 Ⓐ Ⓑ Ⓒ Ⓓ Ⓔ	27 Ⓐ Ⓑ Ⓒ Ⓓ Ⓔ
8 Ⓐ Ⓑ Ⓒ Ⓓ Ⓔ	18 Ⓐ Ⓑ Ⓒ Ⓓ Ⓔ	28 Ⓐ Ⓑ Ⓒ Ⓓ Ⓔ
9 Ⓐ Ⓑ Ⓒ Ⓓ Ⓔ	19 Ⓐ Ⓑ Ⓒ Ⓓ Ⓔ	29 Ⓐ Ⓑ Ⓒ Ⓓ Ⓔ
10 Ⓐ Ⓑ Ⓒ Ⓓ Ⓔ	20 Ⓐ Ⓑ Ⓒ Ⓓ Ⓔ	30 Ⓐ Ⓑ Ⓒ Ⓓ Ⓔ

Name _____ Date _____

Practice Test 3: Problem Solving

Directions. Choose the best answer to each question. Mark your answer. If the correct answer is *not given*, choose "NG."

1 Mr. Cole picked **125** apples and **68** pears from the trees in his yard.

125   **68**

How many fruits did he pick in all?

Ⓐ 203
Ⓑ 193
Ⓒ 183
Ⓓ 57
Ⓔ NG

2 Eliza had **320** ears of corn to sell at her farm stand. By the end of the day, she had sold **275** ears. How many ears of corn were left?

Ⓐ 595
Ⓑ 155
Ⓒ 45
Ⓓ 35
Ⓔ NG

3 Mr. Wagner plans to drive **640** miles to Los Angeles. He has gone **492** miles so far. How many more miles does he have to go?

Ⓐ 252
Ⓑ 248
Ⓒ 158
Ⓓ 152
Ⓔ NG

4 Henry practices playing the piano for 15 minutes each day. How much time does he spend practicing in 5 days?

Ⓐ 20 minutes
Ⓑ 55 minutes
Ⓒ 75 minutes
Ⓓ 90 minutes
Ⓔ NG

5 Five friends will share a bag of peanuts equally. There are **30** peanuts in the bag. How many peanuts will each person get?

Ⓐ 6
Ⓑ 7
Ⓒ 8
Ⓓ 9
Ⓔ NG

GO ON

Practice Test 3 *(continued)*

6 Kelly bought a gallon of milk for **$3.94**. She paid for it with a **$5** bill.

$3.94

How much change should she get?

Ⓐ $0.06
Ⓑ $0.60
Ⓒ $0.96
Ⓓ $1.06
Ⓔ NG

7 Mike bought a set of markers for **$2.85**. The tax was **$0.16**.

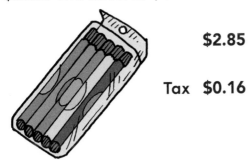

$2.85

Tax $0.16

What was the total cost of the markers?

Ⓐ $2.01
Ⓑ $2.68
Ⓒ $2.91
Ⓓ $3.05
Ⓔ NG

8 Abby's soccer game started at the time shown.

The game ended 1 hour 15 minutes later. What time did the game end?

Ⓐ 4:30
Ⓑ 4:45
Ⓒ 5:00
Ⓓ 5:15
Ⓔ NG

9 Jamie went to a fair and bought a book of **50** tickets. Each ride takes **4** or **5** tickets. <u>About</u> how many rides can he take?

Ⓐ 5
Ⓑ 10
Ⓒ 20
Ⓓ 40

10 Kim wants to buy a game system that costs **$198**. She has saved **$47** so far. <u>About</u> how much more money does she need?

Ⓐ $50
Ⓑ $100
Ⓒ $150
Ⓓ $200

Practice Test 3 *(continued)*

11 Jim is playing a game with this spinner.

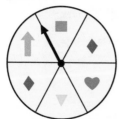

If he spins the spinner **10** times, what will he spin most often?

Ⓐ ◆

Ⓑ ♥

Ⓒ ■

Ⓓ ↑

Ⓔ NG

12 Pia has these colored blocks in a box.

Color	Number of Blocks
Red	9
Yellow	8
Blue	4
Green	6
Orange	12

If Pia takes one block out of the box without looking, she is most likely to get what color?

Ⓐ red

Ⓑ yellow

Ⓒ green

Ⓓ orange

Ⓔ NG

13 Jo read **3** books last week. Dale read **1** more than Jo. Sam read twice as many books as Dale. How many books did Sam read?

Ⓐ 3

Ⓑ 4

Ⓒ 6

Ⓓ 8

Ⓔ NG

14 Tammy had **43** picture books. She gave **16** books to her little brother. Which number sentence should be used to find how many books she has left?

Ⓐ $43 - 16 = \square$

Ⓑ $43 + 16 = \square$

Ⓒ $16 - 43 = \square$

Ⓓ $43 \times 16 = \square$

Ⓔ NG

15 Mr. Lane bought **6** cases of soda. Each case has **24** cans. Which number sentence should be used to find how many cans of soda he bought in all?

Ⓐ $24 - 6 = \square$

Ⓑ $6 + 24 = \square$

Ⓒ $6 \times 24 = \square$

Ⓓ $24 \div 6 = \square$

Ⓔ NG

GO ON

Practice Test 3 *(continued)*

16 Tim has a job as a babysitter. Last week he baby-sat for **5** hours. What else do you need to know to find how much money Tim made?

(A) the name of the family he worked for

(B) how much he was paid per hour

(C) where he baby-sat

(D) how many kids he baby-sat

(E) NG

17 Ms. Jones bought these things at the store.

$24.50   **$8.00**

She gave the clerk **$40.00**. How much change should she get?

(A) $6.50

(B) $7.50

(C) $16.50

(D) $32.50

(E) NG

18 Joey weighed **100** pounds on January 1st. He gained **6** pounds in January and **5** pounds in February. In March he lost **4** pounds. How much did Joey weigh at the end of March?

(A) 101 pounds

(B) 108 pounds

(C) 111 pounds

(D) 115 pounds

(E) NG

19 A group of children went to the aquarium. There were **7** children in one van and **8** children in another van.

Tickets for the aquarium were **$4.00** each.

How much did the tickets cost for all the children together?

(A) $15.00

(B) $19.00

(C) $40.00

(D) $60.00

(E) NG

Answer Sheet

Practice Test 3

Student Name _____

Grade _____

Teacher Name _____

Date _____

MATHEMATICS

1 Ⓐ Ⓑ Ⓒ Ⓓ Ⓔ	11 Ⓐ Ⓑ Ⓒ Ⓓ Ⓔ	21 Ⓐ Ⓑ Ⓒ Ⓓ Ⓔ
2 Ⓐ Ⓑ Ⓒ Ⓓ Ⓔ	12 Ⓐ Ⓑ Ⓒ Ⓓ Ⓔ	22 Ⓐ Ⓑ Ⓒ Ⓓ Ⓔ
3 Ⓐ Ⓑ Ⓒ Ⓓ Ⓔ	13 Ⓐ Ⓑ Ⓒ Ⓓ Ⓔ	23 Ⓐ Ⓑ Ⓒ Ⓓ Ⓔ
4 Ⓐ Ⓑ Ⓒ Ⓓ Ⓔ	14 Ⓐ Ⓑ Ⓒ Ⓓ Ⓔ	24 Ⓐ Ⓑ Ⓒ Ⓓ Ⓔ
5 Ⓐ Ⓑ Ⓒ Ⓓ Ⓔ	15 Ⓐ Ⓑ Ⓒ Ⓓ Ⓔ	25 Ⓐ Ⓑ Ⓒ Ⓓ Ⓔ
6 Ⓐ Ⓑ Ⓒ Ⓓ Ⓔ	16 Ⓐ Ⓑ Ⓒ Ⓓ Ⓔ	26 Ⓐ Ⓑ Ⓒ Ⓓ Ⓔ
7 Ⓐ Ⓑ Ⓒ Ⓓ Ⓔ	17 Ⓐ Ⓑ Ⓒ Ⓓ Ⓔ	27 Ⓐ Ⓑ Ⓒ Ⓓ Ⓔ
8 Ⓐ Ⓑ Ⓒ Ⓓ Ⓔ	18 Ⓐ Ⓑ Ⓒ Ⓓ Ⓔ	28 Ⓐ Ⓑ Ⓒ Ⓓ Ⓔ
9 Ⓐ Ⓑ Ⓒ Ⓓ Ⓔ	19 Ⓐ Ⓑ Ⓒ Ⓓ Ⓔ	29 Ⓐ Ⓑ Ⓒ Ⓓ Ⓔ
10 Ⓐ Ⓑ Ⓒ Ⓓ Ⓔ	20 Ⓐ Ⓑ Ⓒ Ⓓ Ⓔ	30 Ⓐ Ⓑ Ⓒ Ⓓ Ⓔ

Name ______________________________ Date ______________

Practice Test 4: Computation

Directions. Choose the best answer to each question. Mark your answer. If the correct answer is *not given*, choose "NG."

1

$$\begin{array}{r} 215 \\ +\ 67 \\ \hline \end{array}$$

Ⓐ 292
Ⓑ 282
Ⓒ 281
Ⓓ 272
Ⓔ NG

2 **This chart shows the number of shirts sold at a clothing store in one day.**

Shirts Sold	
T-Shirts	12
Boys' Shirts	20
Sweatshirts	8
Girls' Shirts	14

How many shirts were sold in all that day?

Ⓐ 32
Ⓑ 40
Ⓒ 42
Ⓓ 54
Ⓔ NG

3

$$\begin{array}{r} 248 \\ -\ 95 \\ \hline \end{array}$$

Ⓐ 343
Ⓑ 163
Ⓒ 153
Ⓓ 152
Ⓔ NG

4 $6 \times 5 = \square$

Ⓐ 24
Ⓑ 28
Ⓒ 30
Ⓓ 35
Ⓔ NG

5

$$\begin{array}{r} 42 \\ \times\ \ 3 \\ \hline \end{array}$$

Ⓐ 18
Ⓑ 26
Ⓒ 45
Ⓓ 125
Ⓔ NG

6 $28 \times 10 = \square$

Ⓐ 280
Ⓑ 281
Ⓒ 290
Ⓓ 2810
Ⓔ NG

GO ON

Name _____   Date _____

Practice Test 4 *(continued)*

7 The chart shows the number of students who went to swim lessons each day.

Students at Swim Lessons	
Monday	6
Wednesday	9
Friday	15

What was the average number of students at swim lessons each day?

Ⓐ 30
Ⓑ 10
Ⓒ 7
Ⓓ 6
Ⓔ NG

8 $6\overline{)42}$

Ⓐ 4
Ⓑ 5
Ⓒ 6
Ⓓ 7
Ⓔ NG

9 $18 \div 3 = \square$

Ⓐ 3
Ⓑ 4
Ⓒ 5
Ⓓ 8
Ⓔ NG

10
$$\begin{array}{r} \frac{1}{4} \\ + \frac{1}{4} \\ \hline \end{array}$$

Ⓐ $\frac{2}{8}$
Ⓑ $\frac{1}{8}$
Ⓒ $\frac{1}{2}$
Ⓓ $\frac{1}{3}$
Ⓔ NG

11 Hank has **3** pairs of socks and **4** pairs of sneakers.

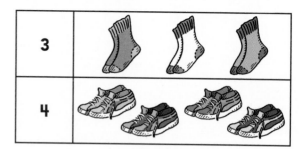

How many different combinations of **1** pair of socks and **1** pair of sneakers can he make?

Ⓐ 15
Ⓑ 12
Ⓒ 7
Ⓓ 3
Ⓔ NG

GO ON

Practice Test 4 *(continued)*

12 Jenna has these fruits in a bag.

If she takes one fruit without looking, what kind is it most likely to be?

(A)

(B)

(C)

(D)

(E) NG

13 $\frac{2}{3} - \frac{1}{3} = \square$

    (A) $\frac{1}{3}$

    (B) $\frac{3}{6}$

    (C) $\frac{1}{6}$

    (D) $\frac{2}{9}$

    (E) NG

14
$$\begin{array}{r} \$6.50 \\ + \ 3.75 \\ \hline \end{array}$$

    (A) $10.75
    (B) $10.25
    (C) $9.25
    (D) $3.25
    (E) NG

15 $1.2 + 3.4 = \square$

    (A) 2.2
    (B) 3.6
    (C) 4.6
    (D) 4.8
    (E) NG

16 Mickey rode **8.4** miles on his bike in the morning. Then he rode **5.5** miles in the afternoon.

| 8.4 miles | Morning |
| 5.5 miles | Afternoon |

How far did Mickey ride in all?

    (A) 3.9 miles
    (B) 4.9 miles
    (C) 13.1 miles
    (D) 13.9 miles
    (E) NG

GO ON ⟹

Practice Test 4 *(continued)*

17 $6 + \square = 15$

What number goes in the box to make the sentence true?

Ⓐ 7

Ⓑ 8

Ⓒ 9

Ⓓ 10

Ⓔ NG

18 $12 - n = 10$

What is the value of n?

Ⓐ 2

Ⓑ 3

Ⓒ 4

Ⓓ 5

Ⓔ NG

19 $7 \times \square = 21$

What number goes in the box?

Ⓐ 2

Ⓑ 3

Ⓒ 4

Ⓓ 6

Ⓔ NG

Use the grid below to answer questions 20 and 21.

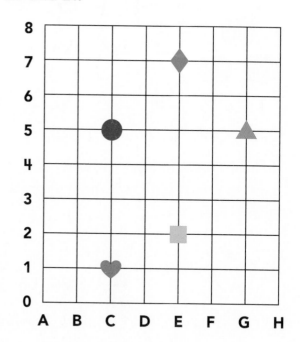

20 Where is the ▢ located?

Ⓐ C, 1

Ⓑ E, 2

Ⓒ G, 5

Ⓓ E, 7

Ⓔ NG

21 What is located at C5?

Ⓐ ♥

Ⓑ ▲

Ⓒ ◆

Ⓓ ●

Ⓔ NG

STOP

Answer Sheet

Student Name _____

Grade _____

Teacher Name _____

Date _____

MATHEMATICS

1 Ⓐ Ⓑ Ⓒ Ⓓ Ⓔ	11 Ⓐ Ⓑ Ⓒ Ⓓ Ⓔ	21 Ⓐ Ⓑ Ⓒ Ⓓ Ⓔ
2 Ⓐ Ⓑ Ⓒ Ⓓ Ⓔ	12 Ⓐ Ⓑ Ⓒ Ⓓ Ⓔ	22 Ⓐ Ⓑ Ⓒ Ⓓ Ⓔ
3 Ⓐ Ⓑ Ⓒ Ⓓ Ⓔ	13 Ⓐ Ⓑ Ⓒ Ⓓ Ⓔ	23 Ⓐ Ⓑ Ⓒ Ⓓ Ⓔ
4 Ⓐ Ⓑ Ⓒ Ⓓ Ⓔ	14 Ⓐ Ⓑ Ⓒ Ⓓ Ⓔ	24 Ⓐ Ⓑ Ⓒ Ⓓ Ⓔ
5 Ⓐ Ⓑ Ⓒ Ⓓ Ⓔ	15 Ⓐ Ⓑ Ⓒ Ⓓ Ⓔ	25 Ⓐ Ⓑ Ⓒ Ⓓ Ⓔ
6 Ⓐ Ⓑ Ⓒ Ⓓ Ⓔ	16 Ⓐ Ⓑ Ⓒ Ⓓ Ⓔ	26 Ⓐ Ⓑ Ⓒ Ⓓ Ⓔ
7 Ⓐ Ⓑ Ⓒ Ⓓ Ⓔ	17 Ⓐ Ⓑ Ⓒ Ⓓ Ⓔ	27 Ⓐ Ⓑ Ⓒ Ⓓ Ⓔ
8 Ⓐ Ⓑ Ⓒ Ⓓ Ⓔ	18 Ⓐ Ⓑ Ⓒ Ⓓ Ⓔ	28 Ⓐ Ⓑ Ⓒ Ⓓ Ⓔ
9 Ⓐ Ⓑ Ⓒ Ⓓ Ⓔ	19 Ⓐ Ⓑ Ⓒ Ⓓ Ⓔ	29 Ⓐ Ⓑ Ⓒ Ⓓ Ⓔ
10 Ⓐ Ⓑ Ⓒ Ⓓ Ⓔ	20 Ⓐ Ⓑ Ⓒ Ⓓ Ⓔ	30 Ⓐ Ⓑ Ⓒ Ⓓ Ⓔ

Practice Test 5: Numeration and Number Concepts

Directions. Choose the best answer to each question. Mark your answer.

1 Mr. Crowley was counting pairs of children on a school bus.

> . . . **6, 8, 10, 12,** ___

Which number should come next?

Ⓐ 13
Ⓑ 14
Ⓒ 15
Ⓓ 16

2 There are **10** flowers in each bunch.

How many flowers are there in all?

Ⓐ 8
Ⓑ 50
Ⓒ 53
Ⓓ 54

3 Ms. Grimes wrote a check for three thousand nine hundred ten dollars. Which number means three thousand nine hundred ten?

Ⓐ 3091
Ⓑ 3901
Ⓒ 3910
Ⓓ 30,910

4 Cheaha Mountain in Alabama is about **2405** feet high. What is that number in words?

Ⓐ two thousand four hundred five
Ⓑ two thousand forty-five
Ⓒ two thousand four hundred fifty
Ⓓ two hundred forty-five

5 Which address is an even number?

Ⓐ 31 Mill Road
Ⓑ 45 First Avenue
Ⓒ 59 Cane Road
Ⓓ 60 Brook Street

GO ON ➡

Practice Test 5 *(continued)*

6 The chart shows the length of four bridges in Texas.

Bridges	Length (feet)
Neches River	673
Trinity River	1870
Ship Channel	1575
Martin Luther King	5032

Which bridge is longest?

Ⓐ Neches River

Ⓑ Trinity River

Ⓒ Ship Channel

Ⓓ Martin Luther King

7 The chart shows the height of four dams in the United States.

Dam	Height (feet)
Dworshak	717
Glen Canyon	710
Hoover	726
Oroville	770

Which dam is highest?

Ⓐ Dworshak

Ⓑ Glen Canyon

Ⓒ Hoover

Ⓓ Oroville

8 Which number means

2000 + 70 + 3 ?

Ⓐ 273

Ⓑ 2073

Ⓒ 2703

Ⓓ 20,703

9 A total of **2945** people went to a hockey game. What does the **4** stand for in **2945**?

Ⓐ 4 thousands

Ⓑ 4 hundreds

Ⓒ 4 tens

Ⓓ 4 ones

10 There are **3689** people living in the town of Wingate. What is that number rounded to the nearest hundred?

Ⓐ 3000

Ⓑ 3700

Ⓒ 3800

Ⓓ 4000

GO ON

Practice Test 5 (continued)

11 Ms. Welles is making a quilt with this pattern.

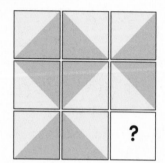

What goes in the blank square to complete the pattern?

12 Doreen made this number pattern.

2, 7, 12, 17, ___

If the same pattern continues, what number should come next?

Ⓐ 18
Ⓑ 20
Ⓒ 22
Ⓓ 24

13 Which sign has an odd number?

14 Which number is marked on the number line?

Ⓐ 38   Ⓒ 35
Ⓑ 36   Ⓓ 33

15 Dolly's Bakery sold **512** muffins on Friday and **684** muffins on Saturday. <u>About</u> how many muffins were sold in those two days?

Ⓐ 1200
Ⓑ 1400
Ⓒ 1600
Ⓓ 1800

GO ON

Practice Test 5 *(continued)*

16 What number is shown on the number line?

300   400↑   500

Ⓐ 342

Ⓑ 402

Ⓒ 412

Ⓓ 420

17 Becca got **$97.00** for her birthday. She spent **$48.00** for a new baseball glove. <u>About</u> how much money did she have left?

Ⓐ $100

Ⓑ $50

Ⓒ $30

Ⓓ $10

18 Which is another way to write

8 + 8 + 8 ?

Ⓐ 3 × 8

Ⓑ 8 + 3

Ⓒ 8 × 8 × 8

Ⓓ 24 + 8

19 Polly got these fish at the pet shop.

What fractional part of these fish are black?

Ⓐ $\frac{3}{5}$ Ⓒ $\frac{2}{1}$

Ⓑ $\frac{2}{3}$ Ⓓ $\frac{2}{5}$

20 Which number goes in the box to make this number sentence true?

9 × 0 = ☐

Ⓐ 0   Ⓒ 9

Ⓑ 1   Ⓓ 90

21 Which bag of peanuts weighs most?

Ⓐ 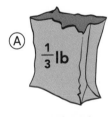 $\frac{1}{3}$ lb

Ⓒ 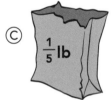 $\frac{1}{5}$ lb

Ⓑ 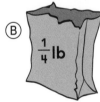 $\frac{1}{4}$ lb

Ⓓ 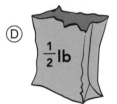 $\frac{1}{2}$ lb

STOP

Answer Sheet

Practice Test 5

Student Name _____ Grade _____

Teacher Name _____ Date _____

MATHEMATICS

1 Ⓐ Ⓑ Ⓒ Ⓓ Ⓔ   11 Ⓐ Ⓑ Ⓒ Ⓓ Ⓔ   21 Ⓐ Ⓑ Ⓒ Ⓓ Ⓔ
2 Ⓐ Ⓑ Ⓒ Ⓓ Ⓔ   12 Ⓐ Ⓑ Ⓒ Ⓓ Ⓔ   22 Ⓐ Ⓑ Ⓒ Ⓓ Ⓔ
3 Ⓐ Ⓑ Ⓒ Ⓓ Ⓔ   13 Ⓐ Ⓑ Ⓒ Ⓓ Ⓔ   23 Ⓐ Ⓑ Ⓒ Ⓓ Ⓔ
4 Ⓐ Ⓑ Ⓒ Ⓓ Ⓔ   14 Ⓐ Ⓑ Ⓒ Ⓓ Ⓔ   24 Ⓐ Ⓑ Ⓒ Ⓓ Ⓔ
5 Ⓐ Ⓑ Ⓒ Ⓓ Ⓔ   15 Ⓐ Ⓑ Ⓒ Ⓓ Ⓔ   25 Ⓐ Ⓑ Ⓒ Ⓓ Ⓔ
6 Ⓐ Ⓑ Ⓒ Ⓓ Ⓔ   16 Ⓐ Ⓑ Ⓒ Ⓓ Ⓔ   26 Ⓐ Ⓑ Ⓒ Ⓓ Ⓔ
7 Ⓐ Ⓑ Ⓒ Ⓓ Ⓔ   17 Ⓐ Ⓑ Ⓒ Ⓓ Ⓔ   27 Ⓐ Ⓑ Ⓒ Ⓓ Ⓔ
8 Ⓐ Ⓑ Ⓒ Ⓓ Ⓔ   18 Ⓐ Ⓑ Ⓒ Ⓓ Ⓔ   28 Ⓐ Ⓑ Ⓒ Ⓓ Ⓔ
9 Ⓐ Ⓑ Ⓒ Ⓓ Ⓔ   19 Ⓐ Ⓑ Ⓒ Ⓓ Ⓔ   29 Ⓐ Ⓑ Ⓒ Ⓓ Ⓔ
10 Ⓐ Ⓑ Ⓒ Ⓓ Ⓔ   20 Ⓐ Ⓑ Ⓒ Ⓓ Ⓔ   30 Ⓐ Ⓑ Ⓒ Ⓓ Ⓔ

© Scholastic Inc.

Practice Test 6: Geometry and Measurement

Directions. Choose the best answer to each question. Mark your answer.

1 Which figure is a rectangle?

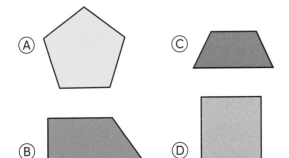

2 Which is shaped like a cone?

3 If you fold each figure on the dotted line, in which figure will the two halves match exactly?

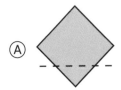
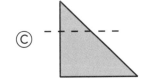
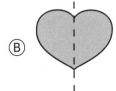
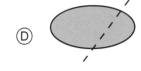

4 Fran made this square.

How many of these squares will fit into this figure?

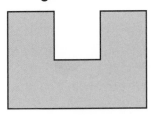

Ⓐ 3   Ⓒ 6
Ⓑ 5   Ⓓ 8

5 Jared has these coins in his pocket.

How much money does Jared have in his pocket?

Ⓐ 28¢
Ⓑ 37¢
Ⓒ 42¢
Ⓓ 46¢

GO ON

Practice Test 6 *(continued)*

6 May Li got this much change back at the store.

How much change did she get?

Ⓐ $1.30
Ⓑ $2.06
Ⓒ $2.30
Ⓓ $2.35

7 What is the area of this figure (in square units)?

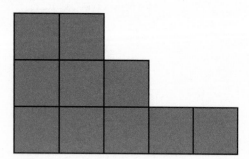

Ⓐ 12
Ⓑ 10
Ⓒ 8
Ⓓ 6

8 Glen woke up at the time shown on the clock.

What time did Glen wake up?

Ⓐ 6:45
Ⓑ 7:00
Ⓒ 7:15
Ⓓ 7:45

9 Debbie's swim lessons started at the time shown on the clock.

Which clock face shows the same time?

Ⓐ    Ⓒ

Ⓑ    Ⓓ

GO ON

Practice Test 6 *(continued)*

10 Which unit should be used to measure the length of a classroom?

Ⓐ miles

Ⓑ pounds

Ⓒ feet

Ⓓ gallons

11 Danny put some milk in a bowl for his cat. If he measured the amount of milk in the bowl, it would be about —

Ⓐ 5 ounces

Ⓑ 5 cups

Ⓒ 5 yards

Ⓓ 5 quarts

12 How long is the pencil? (Use your inch ruler.)

Ⓐ 2 inches

Ⓑ 3 inches

Ⓒ 4 inches

Ⓓ 5 inches

13 How long is the stick of gum? (Use your centimeter ruler.)

Ⓐ 5 centimeters

Ⓑ 6 centimeters

Ⓒ 7 centimeters

Ⓓ 8 centimeters

14 Hannah went swimming in the lake on a summer day. What was most likely the temperature that day?

Ⓐ 32°F

Ⓑ 60°F

Ⓒ 40°F

Ⓓ 85°F

15 Which two figures are the same size and shape?

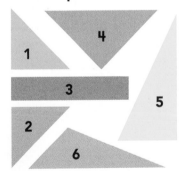

Ⓐ 1 and 2

Ⓑ 3 and 6

Ⓒ 5 and 6

Ⓓ 4 and 5

GO ON

Practice Test 6 *(continued)*

16 Where is the ◆ located on the grid?

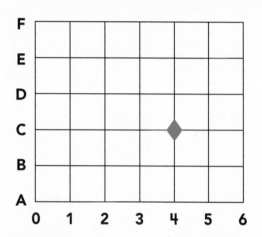

Ⓐ 4, D   Ⓒ 4, C

Ⓑ 3, D   Ⓓ 4, E

17 This tile was turned on its side in the direction of the arrow.

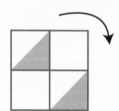

Which picture shows the tile after it was turned?

Ⓐ   Ⓒ

Ⓑ   Ⓓ

Adele made a graph to show how many books she read each week. Use the graph to answer questions 18 and 19.

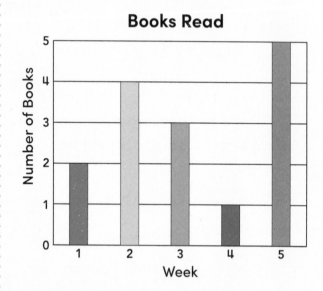

18 In which week did Adele read the most books?

Ⓐ Week 2

Ⓑ Week 3

Ⓒ Week 4

Ⓓ Week 5

19 How many books did she read in Week 2?

Ⓐ 5

Ⓑ 4

Ⓒ 3

Ⓓ 2

STOP

Answer Sheet

Student Name _____ Grade _____

Teacher Name _____ Date _____

MATHEMATICS

1 Ⓐ Ⓑ Ⓒ Ⓓ Ⓔ	11 Ⓐ Ⓑ Ⓒ Ⓓ Ⓔ	21 Ⓐ Ⓑ Ⓒ Ⓓ Ⓔ
2 Ⓐ Ⓑ Ⓒ Ⓓ Ⓔ	12 Ⓐ Ⓑ Ⓒ Ⓓ Ⓔ	22 Ⓐ Ⓑ Ⓒ Ⓓ Ⓔ
3 Ⓐ Ⓑ Ⓒ Ⓓ Ⓔ	13 Ⓐ Ⓑ Ⓒ Ⓓ Ⓔ	23 Ⓐ Ⓑ Ⓒ Ⓓ Ⓔ
4 Ⓐ Ⓑ Ⓒ Ⓓ Ⓔ	14 Ⓐ Ⓑ Ⓒ Ⓓ Ⓔ	24 Ⓐ Ⓑ Ⓒ Ⓓ Ⓔ
5 Ⓐ Ⓑ Ⓒ Ⓓ Ⓔ	15 Ⓐ Ⓑ Ⓒ Ⓓ Ⓔ	25 Ⓐ Ⓑ Ⓒ Ⓓ Ⓔ
6 Ⓐ Ⓑ Ⓒ Ⓓ Ⓔ	16 Ⓐ Ⓑ Ⓒ Ⓓ Ⓔ	26 Ⓐ Ⓑ Ⓒ Ⓓ Ⓔ
7 Ⓐ Ⓑ Ⓒ Ⓓ Ⓔ	17 Ⓐ Ⓑ Ⓒ Ⓓ Ⓔ	27 Ⓐ Ⓑ Ⓒ Ⓓ Ⓔ
8 Ⓐ Ⓑ Ⓒ Ⓓ Ⓔ	18 Ⓐ Ⓑ Ⓒ Ⓓ Ⓔ	28 Ⓐ Ⓑ Ⓒ Ⓓ Ⓔ
9 Ⓐ Ⓑ Ⓒ Ⓓ Ⓔ	19 Ⓐ Ⓑ Ⓒ Ⓓ Ⓔ	29 Ⓐ Ⓑ Ⓒ Ⓓ Ⓔ
10 Ⓐ Ⓑ Ⓒ Ⓓ Ⓔ	20 Ⓐ Ⓑ Ⓒ Ⓓ Ⓔ	30 Ⓐ Ⓑ Ⓒ Ⓓ Ⓔ

Practice Test 7: Problem Solving

Directions. Choose the best answer to each question. Mark your answer. If the correct answer is *not given*, choose "NG."

1 At a pet show, there were **119** dogs and **85** cats.

119   **85**

How many animals in all were at the pet show?

Ⓐ 214
Ⓑ 204
Ⓒ 198
Ⓓ 194
Ⓔ NG

2 Mike has several books on different topics.

Dinosaurs	15
Airplanes	8
Sports	11

How many books does he have in all?

Ⓐ 19
Ⓑ 23
Ⓒ 26
Ⓓ 35
Ⓔ NG

3 Carol is reading a book that is **360** pages long. She has read **219** pages so far. How many pages does she have left to read?

Ⓐ 579
Ⓑ 159
Ⓒ 141
Ⓓ 131
Ⓔ NG

4 Glenn exercises for **25** minutes each day, **5** days each week. How much time does he spend exercising each week?

Ⓐ 30 minutes
Ⓑ 105 minutes
Ⓒ 120 minutes
Ⓓ 125 minutes
Ⓔ NG

5 A school has **6** vans, and **7** students can ride in each van. How many students in all can ride in the vans?

Ⓐ 48
Ⓑ 42
Ⓒ 35
Ⓓ 13
Ⓔ NG

GO ON

Practice Test 7 *(continued)*

6 Ms. Lopez is making **205** cupcakes for a bake sale. She has made **68** cupcakes so far. <u>About</u> how many more cupcakes does she have to make?

Ⓐ 170
Ⓑ 90
Ⓒ 130
Ⓓ 70

7 Kiki bought lunch for **$8.57**. She paid for it with a **$10** bill. How much change should she get?

Ⓐ $1.48
Ⓑ $1.46
Ⓒ $1.38
Ⓓ $0.48
Ⓔ NG

8 Kent bought a book for **$6.25**. The tax was **$0.38**.

$6.25
Tax $0.38

What was the total cost for the book?

Ⓐ $5.87
Ⓑ $6.53
Ⓒ $6.63
Ⓓ $6.73
Ⓔ NG

9 Ms. Coombs is watching a TV show that lasts **60** minutes. She has been watching for **48** minutes. How much longer will the show last?

Ⓐ 10 minutes
Ⓑ 14 minutes
Ⓒ 22 minutes
Ⓓ 24 minutes
Ⓔ NG

10 Micah bought these things at the hardware store.

$6.09 $9.85 $3.94

<u>About</u> how much did he spend in all?

Ⓐ $10
Ⓑ $15
Ⓒ $20
Ⓓ $30

GO ON

Practice Test 7 (continued)

11 Mr. Matthews has **28** chairs. He wants to put all the chairs in **4** rows with an equal number of chairs in each row. How many chairs will be in each row?

- Ⓐ 5
- Ⓑ 6
- Ⓒ 8
- Ⓓ 9
- Ⓔ NG

12 Look at the spinner.

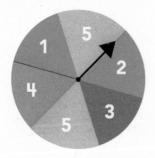

If you spin the spinner once, what number will it most likely land on?

- Ⓐ 5
- Ⓑ 4
- Ⓒ 3
- Ⓓ 2
- Ⓔ NG

13 Pete has these toy ducks in a pool.

Color	Number of Ducks
Yellow	15
White	8
Black	7
Red	6
Blue	10

If Pete takes one duck out of the pool without looking, he is most likely to get which color?

- Ⓐ yellow
- Ⓑ white
- Ⓒ black
- Ⓓ blue
- Ⓔ NG

14 Manny is **48** inches tall. He is **3** inches taller than Kim. Ashley is **3** inches shorter than Kim. How tall is Ashley?

- Ⓐ 46 inches
- Ⓑ 45 inches
- Ⓒ 42 inches
- Ⓓ 39 inches
- Ⓔ NG

GO ON

Name _____ Date _____

Practice Test 7 *(continued)*

15 Tara cut **47** red roses. She sold **28** of them. Which number sentence should be used to find how many roses she had left?

Ⓐ 47 + 28 = ☐
Ⓑ 28 × 47 = ☐
Ⓒ 47 − 28 = ☐
Ⓓ 47 ÷ 28 = ☐
Ⓔ NG

16 Josh bought **5** boxes of golf balls. Each box had **12** balls. Which number sentence should be used to find how many golf balls he bought in all?

Ⓐ 12 + 5 = ☐
Ⓑ 5 × 12 = ☐
Ⓒ 12 − 5 = ☐
Ⓓ 5 + 12 = ☐
Ⓔ NG

17 Karen has a job as a dishwasher in a restaurant. Last week she made a total of **$228.00**. What else do you need to know to find how much Karen makes per hour?

Ⓐ the name of the restaurant
Ⓑ what days she works
Ⓒ when she started her job
Ⓓ how many hours she worked
Ⓔ NG

18 Mr. Ames bought these things at the store.

$25.00 $8.50

He gave the clerk **$50.00**. How much change should he get?

Ⓐ $16.50
Ⓑ $17.50
Ⓒ $25.00
Ⓓ $33.50
Ⓔ NG

19 A family of **2** adults and **3** children went to the discount movie theater. Tickets for adults were **$7.00** each. Tickets for children were **$4.00** each.

How much did the family pay in all for their tickets?

Ⓐ $12.00
Ⓑ $14.00
Ⓒ $26.00
Ⓓ $28.00
Ⓔ NG

STOP

© Scholastic Inc.

Answer Sheet

Student Name _____   Grade _____

Teacher Name _____   Date _____

MATHEMATICS

1	Ⓐ Ⓑ Ⓒ Ⓓ Ⓔ	11	Ⓐ Ⓑ Ⓒ Ⓓ Ⓔ	21	Ⓐ Ⓑ Ⓒ Ⓓ Ⓔ
2	Ⓐ Ⓑ Ⓒ Ⓓ Ⓔ	12	Ⓐ Ⓑ Ⓒ Ⓓ Ⓔ	22	Ⓐ Ⓑ Ⓒ Ⓓ Ⓔ
3	Ⓐ Ⓑ Ⓒ Ⓓ Ⓔ	13	Ⓐ Ⓑ Ⓒ Ⓓ Ⓔ	23	Ⓐ Ⓑ Ⓒ Ⓓ Ⓔ
4	Ⓐ Ⓑ Ⓒ Ⓓ Ⓔ	14	Ⓐ Ⓑ Ⓒ Ⓓ Ⓔ	24	Ⓐ Ⓑ Ⓒ Ⓓ Ⓔ
5	Ⓐ Ⓑ Ⓒ Ⓓ Ⓔ	15	Ⓐ Ⓑ Ⓒ Ⓓ Ⓔ	25	Ⓐ Ⓑ Ⓒ Ⓓ Ⓔ
6	Ⓐ Ⓑ Ⓒ Ⓓ Ⓔ	16	Ⓐ Ⓑ Ⓒ Ⓓ Ⓔ	26	Ⓐ Ⓑ Ⓒ Ⓓ Ⓔ
7	Ⓐ Ⓑ Ⓒ Ⓓ Ⓔ	17	Ⓐ Ⓑ Ⓒ Ⓓ Ⓔ	27	Ⓐ Ⓑ Ⓒ Ⓓ Ⓔ
8	Ⓐ Ⓑ Ⓒ Ⓓ Ⓔ	18	Ⓐ Ⓑ Ⓒ Ⓓ Ⓔ	28	Ⓐ Ⓑ Ⓒ Ⓓ Ⓔ
9	Ⓐ Ⓑ Ⓒ Ⓓ Ⓔ	19	Ⓐ Ⓑ Ⓒ Ⓓ Ⓔ	29	Ⓐ Ⓑ Ⓒ Ⓓ Ⓔ
10	Ⓐ Ⓑ Ⓒ Ⓓ Ⓔ	20	Ⓐ Ⓑ Ⓒ Ⓓ Ⓔ	30	Ⓐ Ⓑ Ⓒ Ⓓ Ⓔ

Practice Test 8: Computation

Directions. Choose the best answer to each question. Mark your answer. If the correct answer is *not given*, choose "NG."

1
$$\begin{array}{r} 405 \\ +\ 98 \\ \hline \end{array}$$

Ⓐ 493
Ⓑ 501
Ⓒ 502
Ⓓ 513
Ⓔ NG

2 This chart shows the number of vegetables picked in one day.

Vegetables Picked	
Carrots	25
Broccoli	14
Cucumbers	16
Squash	8

How many vegetables were picked in all that day?

Ⓐ 39
Ⓑ 53
Ⓒ 55
Ⓓ 63
Ⓔ NG

3 Chuck mowed lawns for three days. This list shows what he earned.

Monday	$24
Tuesday	$28
Wednesday	$13

How much did Chuck earn altogether?

Ⓐ $62
Ⓑ $65
Ⓒ $76
Ⓓ $85
Ⓔ NG

4
$$\begin{array}{r} 329 \\ -\ 57 \\ \hline \end{array}$$

Ⓐ 386
Ⓑ 276
Ⓒ 272
Ⓓ 172
Ⓔ NG

5 $8 \times 5 = \square$

Ⓐ 30
Ⓑ 32
Ⓒ 35
Ⓓ 40
Ⓔ NG

GO ON

Practice Test 8 *(continued)*

6　31
　　× 6

- Ⓐ 186
- Ⓑ 156
- Ⓒ 96
- Ⓓ 37
- Ⓔ NG

7　$15 \times 10 =$ ☐

- Ⓐ 150
- Ⓑ 151
- Ⓒ 160
- Ⓓ 1510
- Ⓔ NG

8 The chart shows the number of points scored in three basketball games.

Points Scored	
Game 1	12
Game 2	8
Game 3	10

What was the average number of points scored per game?

- Ⓐ 8
- Ⓑ 10
- Ⓒ 20
- Ⓓ 30
- Ⓔ NG

9 This chart shows the number of students in a third-grade class with each color of hair.

Color	Number of Students
Black	14
Brown	8
Blond	6
Red	1

If you choose one of these students without looking, the student's hair is most likely to be —

- Ⓐ black
- Ⓒ blond
- Ⓑ brown
- Ⓓ red

10　$7\overline{)35}$

- Ⓐ 4
- Ⓑ 5
- Ⓒ 6
- Ⓓ 7
- Ⓔ NG

11　$24 \div 4 =$ ☐

- Ⓐ 3
- Ⓑ 4
- Ⓒ 5
- Ⓓ 6
- Ⓔ NG

GO ON

Practice Test 8 (continued)

12
$$\begin{array}{r} \frac{1}{2} \\ + \ \frac{1}{2} \\ \hline \end{array}$$

(A) $\frac{1}{4}$

(B) $\frac{2}{3}$

(C) $\frac{2}{4}$

(D) $\frac{3}{4}$

(E) NG

13 Mel has **2** pairs of shorts and **5** T-shirts.

2	
5	

How many different combinations of **1** pair of shorts and **1** T-shirt can she make?

(A) 12

(B) 10

(C) 7

(D) 2

(E) NG

14 $1\frac{1}{2} - \frac{1}{4} = \square$

(A) $\frac{1}{4}$

(B) $\frac{2}{4}$

(C) 1

(D) $1\frac{1}{4}$

(E) NG

15 $6.3 + 1.9 = \square$

(A) 7.1

(B) 7.2

(C) 8.4

(D) 8.6

(E) NG

16 Nancy had **$32.50** in her piggy bank. Then she put in **$4.75** more.

+ $4.75

How much money did she have in all?

(A) $36.25

(B) $36.75

(C) $37.25

(D) $37.75

(E) NG

GO ON →

Practice Test 8 *(continued)*

17

Distance	
Littleton	3.2 km
Ayer	2.5 km

How much farther away is Littleton than Ayer?

Ⓐ 0.7 km

Ⓑ 1.7 km

Ⓒ 5.7 km

Ⓓ 6.0 km

Ⓔ NG

18 $16 + n = 25$
What is the value of n?

Ⓐ 41

Ⓑ 12

Ⓒ 10

Ⓓ 9

Ⓔ NG

19 Which number goes in the box to make the number sentence true?

$$32 - \square = 24$$

Ⓐ 6

Ⓑ 7

Ⓒ 8

Ⓓ 9

Ⓔ NG

Use the grid below to answer questions 20 and 21.

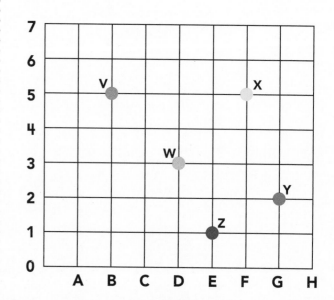

20 What is the location of point Z?

Ⓐ E, 1

Ⓑ D, 3

Ⓒ G, 3

Ⓓ C, 5

Ⓔ NG

21 What is located at F5?

Ⓐ point V

Ⓑ point W

Ⓒ point X

Ⓓ point Y

Ⓔ NG

STOP

Answer Sheet

Student Name _____ Grade _____

Teacher Name _____ Date _____

MATHEMATICS

1 Ⓐ Ⓑ Ⓒ Ⓓ Ⓔ	11 Ⓐ Ⓑ Ⓒ Ⓓ Ⓔ	21 Ⓐ Ⓑ Ⓒ Ⓓ Ⓔ
2 Ⓐ Ⓑ Ⓒ Ⓓ Ⓔ	12 Ⓐ Ⓑ Ⓒ Ⓓ Ⓔ	22 Ⓐ Ⓑ Ⓒ Ⓓ Ⓔ
3 Ⓐ Ⓑ Ⓒ Ⓓ Ⓔ	13 Ⓐ Ⓑ Ⓒ Ⓓ Ⓔ	23 Ⓐ Ⓑ Ⓒ Ⓓ Ⓔ
4 Ⓐ Ⓑ Ⓒ Ⓓ Ⓔ	14 Ⓐ Ⓑ Ⓒ Ⓓ Ⓔ	24 Ⓐ Ⓑ Ⓒ Ⓓ Ⓔ
5 Ⓐ Ⓑ Ⓒ Ⓓ Ⓔ	15 Ⓐ Ⓑ Ⓒ Ⓓ Ⓔ	25 Ⓐ Ⓑ Ⓒ Ⓓ Ⓔ
6 Ⓐ Ⓑ Ⓒ Ⓓ Ⓔ	16 Ⓐ Ⓑ Ⓒ Ⓓ Ⓔ	26 Ⓐ Ⓑ Ⓒ Ⓓ Ⓔ
7 Ⓐ Ⓑ Ⓒ Ⓓ Ⓔ	17 Ⓐ Ⓑ Ⓒ Ⓓ Ⓔ	27 Ⓐ Ⓑ Ⓒ Ⓓ Ⓔ
8 Ⓐ Ⓑ Ⓒ Ⓓ Ⓔ	18 Ⓐ Ⓑ Ⓒ Ⓓ Ⓔ	28 Ⓐ Ⓑ Ⓒ Ⓓ Ⓔ
9 Ⓐ Ⓑ Ⓒ Ⓓ Ⓔ	19 Ⓐ Ⓑ Ⓒ Ⓓ Ⓔ	29 Ⓐ Ⓑ Ⓒ Ⓓ Ⓔ
10 Ⓐ Ⓑ Ⓒ Ⓓ Ⓔ	20 Ⓐ Ⓑ Ⓒ Ⓓ Ⓔ	30 Ⓐ Ⓑ Ⓒ Ⓓ Ⓔ

TESTED SKILLS

Practice Test 1: Numeration and Number Concepts

Tested Skills	Item Numbers
Count by 2s, 10s	1, 2
Associate numerals and number words	3, 4
Compare and order whole numbers	6
Use place value and rounding	7, 8
Identify patterns	9, 10
Identify odd/even numbers	5, 11
Use number lines	13, 21
Estimation	12, 14
Identify fractional parts	16, 17
Compare and order fractions	19, 20
Use number sentences and operational properties	15, 18

Practice Test 2: Geometry and Measurement

Tested Skills	Item Numbers
Identify plane and solid figures and their parts	6, 8
Recognize symmetry and congruence	7, 9
Find area	10
Recognize value of money	3, 12
Tell time	2, 13
Use appropriate units of measurement	1, 15
Use measurement instruments	16, 17
Estimate measurements	14
Identify transformations	18
Find coordinates on a grid	11
Interpret graphs, tables, charts	4, 5

Practice Test 3: Problem Solving

Tested Skills	Item Numbers
Solve problems involving addition or subtraction	1–3
Solve problems involving multiplication or division	4, 5
Solve problems involving money and time	6–8
Use estimation to solve problems	9, 10
Solve problems involving probability or logic	11–13
Identify steps to solve a problem	14–16
Solve multi-step problems	17–19

Practice Test 4: Computation

Tested Skills	Item Numbers
Add and subtract whole numbers	1–3
Multiply whole numbers	4–6
Divide whole numbers	8, 9
Add and subtract fractions	10, 13
Add and subtract decimals	14–16
Find average, probability, and combinations	7, 11, 12
Solve simple equations	17–19
Find coordinates on a grid	20, 21

Practice Test 5: Numeration and Number Concepts

Tested Skills	Item Numbers
Count by 2s, 10s	1, 2
Associate numerals and number words	3, 4
Compare and order whole numbers	6, 7
Use place value and rounding	8–10
Identify patterns	11, 12
Identify odd/even numbers	5, 13
Use number lines	14, 16
Estimation	15, 17
Identify fractional parts	19
Compare and order fractions	21
Use number sentences and operational properties	18, 20

Practice Test 6: Geometry and Measurement

Tested Skills	Item Numbers
Identify plane and solid figures and their parts	1, 2
Recognize symmetry and congruence	3, 15
Find area	4, 7
Recognize value of money	5, 6
Tell time	8, 9
Use appropriate units of measurement	10, 11
Use measurement instruments	12, 13
Estimate measurements	14
Identify transformations	17
Find coordinates on a grid	16
Interpret graphs, tables, charts	18, 19

Practice Test 7: Problem Solving

Tested Skills	Item Numbers
Solve problems involving addition or subtraction	1–3
Solve problems involving multiplication or division	4, 5, 11
Solve problems involving money and time	7–9
Use estimation to solve problems	6, 10
Solve problems involving probability or logic	12–14
Identify steps to solve a problem	15–17
Solve multi-step problems	18, 19

Practice Test 8: Computation

Tested Skills	Item Numbers
Add and subtract whole numbers	1–4
Multiply whole numbers	5–7
Divide whole numbers	10, 11
Add and subtract fractions	12, 14
Add and subtract decimals	15–17
Find average, probability, and combinations	8, 9, 13
Solve simple equations	18, 19
Find coordinates on a grid	20, 21

ANSWER KEYS

Practice Test 1
Numeration and Number Concepts
1. B   12. C
2. D   13. C
3. D   14. B
4. C   15. D
5. A   16. D
6. B   17. A
7. B   18. B
8. C   19. D
9. A   20. B
10. C   21. B
11. D

Practice Test 2
Geometry and Measurement
1. C   10. A
2. B   11. C
3. A   12. C
4. C   13. B
5. A   14. A
6. A   15. D
7. B   16. B
8. D   17. A
9. B   18. D

Practice Test 3
Problem Solving
1. B   11. A
2. C   12. D
3. E   13. D
4. C   14. A
5. A   15. C
6. D   16. B
7. E   17. B
8. C   18. E
9. B   19. D
10. C

Practice Test 4
Computation
1. B   12. A
2. D   13. A
3. C   14. B
4. C   15. C
5. E   16. D
6. A   17. C
7. B   18. A
8. D   19. B
9. E   20. B
10. C   21. D
11. B

Practice Test 5
Numeration and Number Concepts
1. B   12. C
2. C   13. C
3. C   14. B
4. A   15. A
5. D   16. D
6. D   17. B
7. D   18. A
8. B   19. D
9. C   20. A
10. B   21. D
11. A

Practice Test 6
Geometry and Measurement
1. D   11. A
2. A   12. B
3. B   13. C
4. B   14. D
5. D   15. A
6. C   16. C
7. B   17. A
8. A   18. D
9. D   19. B
10. C

Practice Test 7
Problem Solving
1. B   11. E
2. E   12. A
3. C   13. A
4. D   14. C
5. B   15. C
6. C   16. B
7. E   17. D
8. C   18. A
9. E   19. C
10. C

Practice Test 8
Computation
1. E   12. E
2. D   13. B
3. B   14. D
4. C   15. E
5. D   16. C
6. A   17. A
7. A   18. D
8. B   19. C
9. A   20. A
10. B   21. C
11. D